John Kember

# Piano Sight-Reading 1

## Déchiffrage pour le piano 1
## Vom-Blatt-Spiel auf dem Klavier 1

*A fresh approach / Nouvelle approche*
*Eine erfrischend neue Methode*

ED 12736
ISMN M-2201-2263-7
ISBN 978-1-84761-132-1

www.schott-music.com

Mainz · London · Madrid · New York · Paris · Prague · Tokyo · Toronto
© 2004 SCHOTT MUSIC Ltd, London · Printed in Germany

**Acknowledgments**
We wish to thank: Blackheath Conservatoire of Music, London, Gareth Bucket,
John Caudwell, Tom Dodd, Andrew Haigh, John and Nathan Hayward, David Sams
and Claire Williams for their valued support, advice and encouragement in the production
of this book.

**Remerciements**
Nous tenons à remercier le Conservatoire de Musique de Blackheath (Londres),
Gareth Bucket, John Caudwell, Tom Dodd, Andrew Haigh, John et Nathan Hayward,
David Sams et Claire Williams de leur soutien, leurs conseils et leurs encouragements
inestimables pour le publication de ce recueil.

**Danksagung**
Wir möchten uns bei dem Blackheath Conservatoire of Music, London, Gareth Bucket,
John Caudwell, Tom Dodd, Andrew Haigh, John und Nathan Hayward, David Sams
und Claire Williams für ihre wertvolle Unterstützung, ihren Rat und ihre Bestärkung bei
der Herstellung dieses Buches bedanken.

ED 12736

British Library Cataloguing-in-Publication Data.
A catalogue record for this book is available from the British Library.
ISMN M-2201-2263-7
ISBN 978-1-84761-132-1

© 2004 Schott Music Ltd, London

French translation: Agnès Ausseur
German translation: Ute Corleis
Cover design and layout by www.adamhaystudio.com
Music setting by Jack Thompson
Printed in Germany S&Co. 7872

# Contents
Sommaire/Inhalt

# Preface

Piano Sight-Reading 1 aims to establish good practice and provide an early introduction to the essential skill of sight-reading.

Sight-reading given as 'homework' is of little value unless the result is heard by the teacher. Ideally, sight-reading in some form should become a regular part of a student's routine each time they go to the piano.

This book aims to establish the habit early in a student's piano playing. Of course, names of notes and time values need to be thoroughly known and understood, but equally sight-reading is helped by an awareness of shape and direction. To this end, Part 1 encourages establishing the rhythm of a short example first, while at the same time observing the shape (rise and fall in pitch) and more precisely noticing repeated notes and movement by step and skip. Examples are given in 'Preparation' for the teacher to use.

In Part 1 the basic keys of C, G, F and D major and A and D minor are explored while keeping to movement limited to steps, skips and repeated notes in a 5-note range.

In Part 2 students are encouraged to identify the key for themselves, and the addition of accidentals, dotted notes, simple ties and syncopations occur in the exercises.

Intervals of 4ths and 5ths are also covered in Part 2, which concludes with some pieces using both hands playing together.

All exercises are no longer than 8 bars in length and remain in a 5-note position throughout. Use is made of familiar 5-finger shapes, patterns and sequences, both rhythmic and melodic.

## To the pupil: Why Sight-Reading?

When you are faced with a new piece and asked to play it, whether you are at home, in a lesson, playing to accompany another instrumentalist, or in an audition or examination, there is no one there to help you – except yourself! Sight-reading tests your ability to read the time and notes correctly and to observe the phrasing and dynamics quickly.

The aim in this book is to help you teach yourself. The book gives guidance on what to look for and how best to prepare yourself in a very short time by observing the time and key signatures, and giving your first thoughts to the tempo and rhythm. These short pieces progress gradually to help build up your confidence and observation and enable you to sight-read accurately and to play steadily.

Try to sight-read something new each time you sit at the piano. You will be amazed at how skilled you will become.

Being a good sight-reader is one of the most important skills you can acquire as an instrumentalist.

Think of these as 'mini-pieces' and try to learn each one quickly and correctly, then when you are faced with real sight-reading you will be well equipped to succeed on a first attempt.

*Remember – you are on your own now!*

# Préface

Le propos de ce recueil de déchiffrage pour le piano est fournir une première initiation et un entraînement solide aux principes de la lecture à vue.

Le déchiffrage imposé comme un « travail » ne présente pas grand intérêt s'il n'est supervisé par le maître. L'idéal serait que le déchiffrage prenne régulièrement place dans la routine de travail de l'élève, à chaque fois qu'il se met au piano.

L'objectif est ici d'établir l'habitude de la lecture à vue très tôt dans l'étude du piano. Le déchiffrage suppose, bien sûr, que les noms et les valeurs de notes soient complètement assimilés et compris mais il s'appuie également sur la conscience des contours et le sens de la direction. Pour faciliter cette démarche, la première partie de ce volume incite d'abord à établir le rythme d'un court exemple tout en observant les formes mélodiques (élévation et abaissement de la hauteur du son) et, plus précisément, en repérant les notes répétées et les mouvements en progression par degrés et en progression par sauts de note. Des exemples à l'usage du maître sont donnés dans la rubrique « Préparation ».

La première partie se limite aux tonalités de *do* majeur, *sol* majeur, *fa* majeur, *ré* majeur, *la* mineur et *ré* mineur, aux mouvements continus progressant par degrés, discontinus progressant par sauts de note et aux notes répétées sur une étendue de cinq notes.

La deuxième partie présente des exercices dont l'élève identifiera lui-même la tonalité et contenant des altérations accidentelles, des notes pointées, des liaisons et des syncopes simples, fait intervenir les intervalles de quarte et de quinte et se termine par des morceaux à deux mains ensemble.

Les exercices, comportant au plus huit mesures et ne dépassant pas l'envergure de la position de la main sur cinq notes, recourent aux contours, formules et séquences, rythmiques et mélodiques, usuels dans les configurations pour cinq doigts.

## A l'élève : Pourquoi le déchiffrage ?

Lorsque vous vous trouvez face à un nouveau morceau que l'on vous demande de jouer, que ce soit chez vous, pendant une leçon, pour accompagner un autre instrumentiste ou lors d'une audition ou d'un examen, personne d'autre que vous-même ne peut vous aider! Le déchiffrage met à l'épreuve votre capacité à lire correctement les rythmes et les notes et à observer rapidement le phrasé et les nuances.

Ce recueil se propose de vous aider à vous entraîner vous-même. Il vous oriente sur ce que vous devez repérer et sur la meilleure manière de vous préparer en un très court laps de temps, en sachant observer les indications de mesure et l'armure de la clef, et de vous donner une première idée du tempo et de rythme. Ces pièces brèves, en progressant par étapes, vous feront prendre de l'assurance, aiguiseront vos observations et vous permettront de lire à vue avec aisance.

Efforcez-vous de déchiffrer quelque chose de nouveau chaque fois que vous vous mettez au piano. Vous serez étonné de vos progrès.

Une bonne lecture à vue est l'une des capacités les plus importantes qu'un instrumentiste puisse acquérir.

Considérez ces pages comme des « mini-morceaux » et essayez de les apprendre rapidement et sans erreur, de manière à ce que, devant un véritable déchiffrage, vous soyez bien équipé pour réussir dès la première lecture.

*N'oubliez pas – vous êtes désormais seul !*

# Vorwort

„Vom-Blatt-Spiel auf dem Klavier 1" möchte zu einer guten Übetechnik verhelfen, indem es frühzeitig zur grundlegenden Fähigkeit des Vom-Blatt-Spiels hinführt.

Vom-Blatt-Spiel als ‚Hausaufgabe' aufzugeben hat wenig Sinn, wenn das Ergebnis nicht vom Lehrer überprüft wird. Im Idealfall sollte das Vom-Blatt-Spiel in irgendeiner Form zu einem festen Bestandteil im Übeprogramm des Schülers werden.

Ziel des vorliegenden Buches ist es, diese Gewohnheit von Anfang an in das Klavierspiel des Schülers zu integrieren. Natürlich muss man die Notennamen und Taktarten gründlich kennen und verstehen, aber auch die Entwicklung eines Bewusstseins für Form und Richtung unterstützt das Vom-Blatt-Spiel.

Um das zu erreichen, ermutigt Teil 1 dazu, zuerst den Rhythmus eines kurzen Beispiels sicher einzuüben, während gleichzeitig die Form (Auf-und Abstieg der Tonhöhe) beobachtet wird und so sich wiederholende Noten und schrittweise oder sprunghafte Bewegungen treffsicherer erkannt werden.

Im Abschnitt ‚Vorbereitung' werden dem Lehrer Beispiele an die Hand gegeben.

In Teil 1 werden die Grundtonarten C-, G-, F-und D-Dur sowie a-und d-Moll erkundet, wobei sich die Melodie auf Schritte, Sprünge und sich wiederholende Noten im 5-Ton-Raum beschränkt.

In Teil 2 werden die Schüler dazu ermuntert, die jeweilige Tonart selbst herauszufinden. Zusätzlich tauchen auch Versetzungszeichen, punktierte Noten, einfache Bindungen und Synkopen in den Übungen auf.

Darüber hinaus werden auch die Intervalle Quarte und Quinte abgedeckt. Teil 2 endet dann mit einigen Stücken, in denen beide Hände zusammenspielen.

Keine Übung ist länger als 8 Takte und alle bleiben durchgängig im 5-Ton-Raum. Dabei werden sowohl rhythmisch als auch melodisch vertraute 5-Finger-Figuren, Muster und Sequenzen benutzt.

## An den Schüler: Warum Vom-Blatt-Spiel?

Wenn du mit einem neuen Stück konfrontiert wirst und man dich dazu auffordert, es zu spielen, gibt es niemanden, der dir dabei helfen kann. Dabei ist es auch völlig egal, ob du zu Hause bist, in einer Unterrichtsstunde, gerade einen anderen Instrumentalisten begleitest, in einem Vorspiel oder einer Prüfung – nur du kannst dir selbst helfen! Das Vom-Blatt-Spiel testet deine Fähigkeit, die Taktart und die Noten richtig zu lesen sowie Phrasierungen und Dynamik schnell zu erkennen.

Ziel dieses Buches ist es, dich zum Selbstunterricht anzuleiten. Das Buch zeigt dir, worauf du achten musst und wie du dich in kurzer Zeit am besten vorbereitest: Du solltest die Taktart und die Vorzeichen erkennen und dann zunächst auf das Tempo und den Rhythmus achten. Diese kurzen Stücke steigern sich nur allmählich, um dein Vertrauen und deine Beobachtungsfähigkeit aufzubauen sowie dich dazu zu befähigen, korrekt und fließend vom Blatt zu spielen.

Versuche, jedes Mal, wenn du am Klavier sitzt, etwas Neues vom Blatt zu spielen. Du wirst dich wundern, wie geschickt du werden wirst.

Eine der wichtigsten Fähigkeiten, die man als Instrumentalist erwerben kann, ist die des Vom-Blatt-Spiels.

Behandle die folgenden Übungen als ‚Mini-Stücke' und versuche, jede schnell und fehlerlos zu erlernen. Wenn du dann tatsächlich einmal vom Blatt spielen musst, wirst du gut ausgerüstet sein und gleich beim ersten Versuch Erfolg haben.

*Denk daran – du bist von jetzt an auf dich alleine gestellt!*

# Part 1
## 1ère Partie/Teil 1

8

## **Preparation** Préparation *Vorbereitung*

COUNT 2:
COMPTEZ 2:
ZÄHLE AUF 2:
} 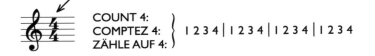 1 2 | 1 2 | 1 2 | 1 2

COUNT 3:
COMPTEZ 3:
ZÄHLE AUF 3:
} 1 2 3 | 1 2 3 | 1 2 3 | 1 2 3

COUNT 4:
COMPTEZ 4:
ZÄHLE AUF 4:
} 1 2 3 4 | 1 2 3 4 | 1 2 3 4 | 1 2 3 4

Movement by STEP links notes of different pitch which alternate between lines and spaces.

La progression continue par degrés relie des notes de hauteurs différentes placées en alternance sur les lignes et dans les interlignes.

Schrittweise Bewegungen verbinden Noten verschiedener Tonhöhe miteinander, die im Notensystem abwechselnd auf Linien und Zwischenräumen stehen.

Movement by SKIP links notes which move from line to line or space to space, 'skipping' over just one note.

La progression discontinue par saut de note relie des notes placées de ligne en ligne ou d'interligne en interligne, « sautant » une note.

Melodische Wendungen, die im Notensystem von Linie zu Linie oder von Zwischenraum zu Zwischenraum fortschreiten, überspringen genau eine Note.

REPEATED NOTES link notes of the same pitch written on the same line or space.

La répétition de notes relie des notes de même hauteur placées sur la même ligne ou dans le même interligne.

Sich wiederholende Noten verbinden Noten der gleichen Tonhöhe miteinander, die auf derselben Linie oder demselben Zwischenraum notiert sind.

# Three Steps to Success
## Trois étapes vers la réussite
### *Drei Schritte zum Erfolg*

1. **Look at the *top* number of the time signature.** It shows the number of beats in the bar. Tap (clap or play on one note) the *rhythm*, counting all the time.

2. **Look for *patterns*.** While tapping the rhythm, look for all the repeated notes and skips. Try to see the shape of the melody – where it rises and falls.

3. *Keep counting steadily as you play*.

1. **Observez le *chiffre supérieur* de l'indication de mesure**, il indique le nombre de pulsations présentes dans chaque mesure. Frappez le rythme (dans les mains ou sur une seule note) en comptant tous les temps.

2. **Recherchez les *formules*.** Tout en frappant le rythme, repérez toutes les notes répétées et les sauts de note. Observez les contours de la mélodie, les endroits où elle monte et descend.

3. *Jouez régulièrement en comptant*.

1. **Schaue dir die *obere Ziffer* der Taktangabe an**. Sie zeigt dir die Anzahl der Schläge innerhalb eines Taktes an. Klopfe (klatsche oder spiele auf 1 Note) den Rhythmus und zähle dabei stets das Metrum.

2. **Halte nach *Mustern* Ausschau**. Während du den Rhythmus klopfst, suche alle sich wiederholenden Noten und Sprünge heraus. Versuche, die Gestalt der Melodie zu erkennen – wo steigt sie an und wo fällt sie ab.

3. *Zähle vollkommen gleichmäßig durch, während du spielst*.

## Patterns: 5-finger shapes and sequences* frequently used
Formules: configurations et séquences*  fréquentes pour 5 doigts
*Muster: 5-Finger-Figuren und häufig benutzte Sequenzen*

* A sequence is a short, repeated melodic phrase which generally rises (or falls) by step.
* Une séquence est une courte phrase mélodique répétée progressant généralement par degrés.
*Eine Sequenz ist eine kurze, sich wiederholende melodische Phrase, die im Normalfall schrittweise an-oder absteigt.

12

**4.**

**5.**

## More patterns to find
Nouvelles formules à découvrir
*Weitere Muster*

Mark with a pencil any shapes or patterns you see repeated.

Entourez au crayon les formules ou contours répétés.

Kennzeichne mit einem Bleistift alle Figuren und Muster, die sich wiederholen.

**1.**

**2.**

**3.**

Count: 1 2 3

14

# Sight-Reading Exercises
## Exercices de lecture à vue
### *Vom-Blatt-Spiel Übungen*

Movement in Part 1 is limited to steps, skips and repeated notes.

Les mouvements mélodiques de la 1ère partie se limitent à la progression par degrés, par sautes de note et aux notes répétées.

Die Bewegungen in Teil 1 beschränken sich auf Schritte, Sprünge und sich wiederholende Noten.

**C major**/*do* majeur/C-Dur

**C major**/*do* majeur/C-Dur

**7.**

**8.**

**9.**

**10.**

**11.**

**C major**/*do* majeur/C-Dur

**12.**

**13.**

**14.**

**15.**

**16.**

**17.**

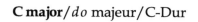 

**C major**/*do* majeur/C-Dur

## 18.

## 19.

## 20.

## 21.

## A New Hand Position
Nouvelle position de la main
*Eine neue Handposition*

**G major**/*sol* majeur/G-Dur

## 1.

**G major**/*sol* majeur/G-Dur

**2.**

**3.**

**4.**

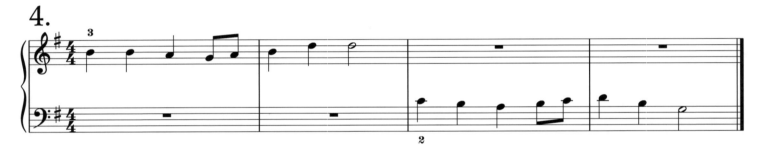

| | | |
|---|---|---|
| These pieces begin on the 4th beat of the bar in 4 time. | Attaque sur le 4ème temps d'une mesure à 4 temps. | Diese Stücke beginnen auf dem vierten Schlag des Taktes im Vierertakt. |
| Count 1-2-3 before you begin. | Comptez 1-2-3 avant d'attaquer. | Zähle 1-2-3, bevor du beginnst. |

**5.**

**6.**

**G major**/*sol* majeur/G-Dur

## 7.

Count 1 2 3

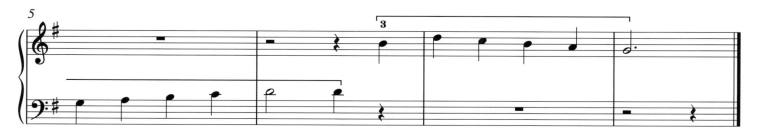

## 8.

Count 1 2 3

| These pieces begin on the 3rd beat of the bar in 3 time. | Attaque sur le 3ème temps d'une mesure à 3 temps. | Dieses Stück beginnt auf dem dritten Schlag des Taktes im Dreiertakt. |
|---|---|---|

## 9.

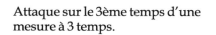

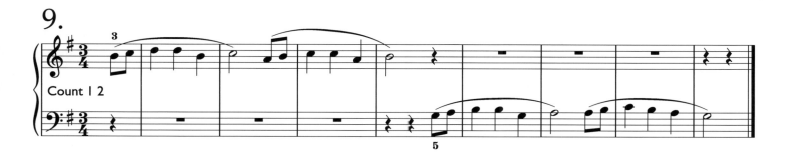

Count 1 2

**G major**/*sol* majeur/G-Dur

### 10.

Count 1 2

### 11.

## A New Hand Position
Nouvelle position de la main
*Eine neue Handposition*

Try to play these slurred note groups smoothly (legato).

Efforcez-vous de jouer les groupes de notes surmontés d'une liaison de façon unie (legato).

Versuche, diese gebundenen Notengruppen fließend zu spielen (legato).

**A minor** /*la* mineur/a-Moll

### 1.

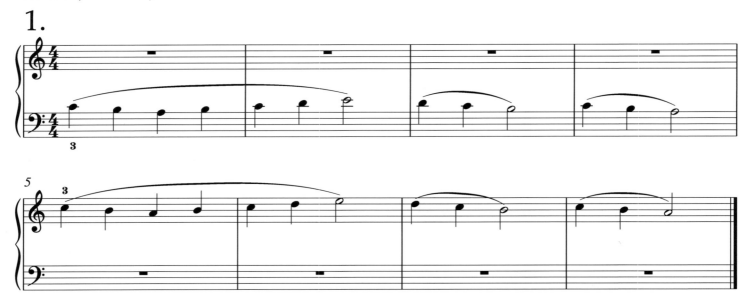

**A minor** / *la* mineur / a-Moll

## 2.

This is in 6/8 time          Mesure à 6/8          Dieses Stück steht im 6/8-Takt

## 3.

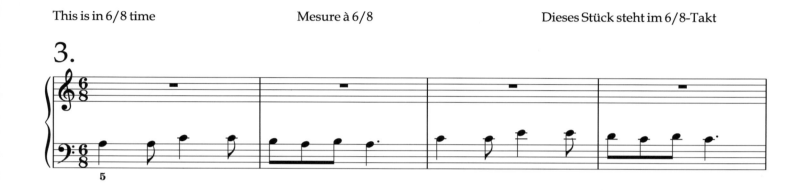

## 4.

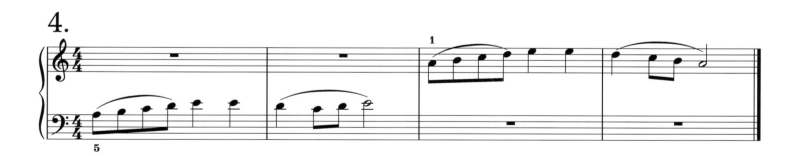

## 5.

22

**A minor** / *la* mineur / a-Moll

## 6.

This begins on the 4th beat of the bar in 4 time.

Attaque sur le 4ème temps d'une mesure à 4 temps.

Dieses Stück beginnt auf dem vierten Schlag des Taktes im Vierertakt.

## 7.

Count 1 2 3

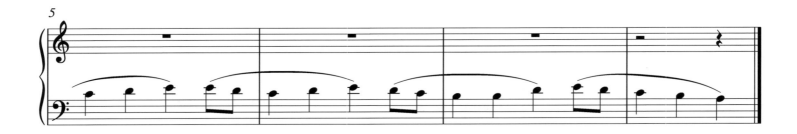

## 8.

**A minor** / *la* mineur / a-Moll

This is in 6/8 time           Mesure à 6/8           Dieses Stück steht im 6/8-Takt

## A New Hand Position
Nouvelle position de la main
*Eine neue Handposition*

**D minor**/*ré* mineur/d-Moll

**1.**

**2.**

**3.**

**D minor**/*ré* mineur/d-Moll

**4.**

**5.**

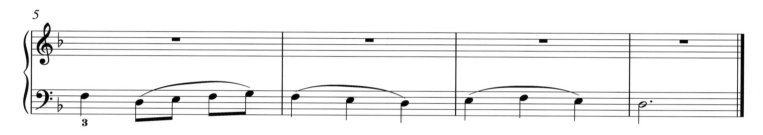

**6.**

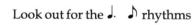 Look out for the ♩. ♪ rhythms     Repérez les rythmes ♩. ♪     Achte auf den ♩. ♪ Rhythmus

**7.**

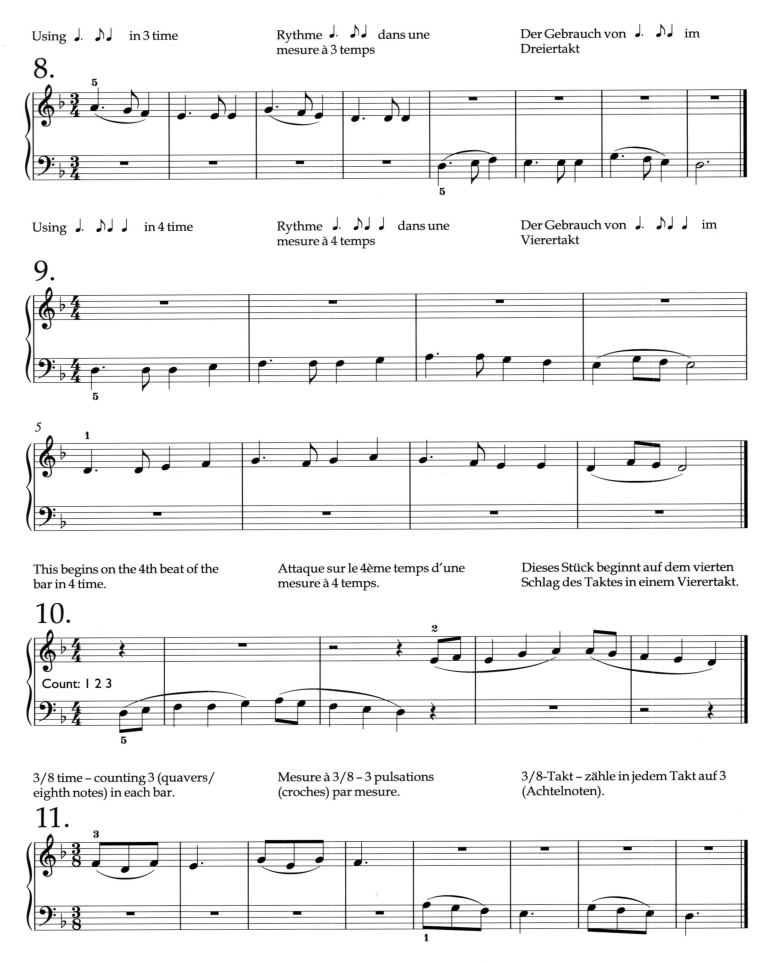

26

**D minor**/*ré* mineur/d-Moll

Using ♩. ♪♪ in 3 time

Rythme ♩. ♪♪ dans une mesure à 3 temps

Der Gebrauch von ♩. ♪♪ im Dreiertakt

**8.**

Using ♩. ♪♪♩ in 4 time

Rythme ♩. ♪♪♩ dans une mesure à 4 temps

Der Gebrauch von ♩. ♪♪♩ im Vierertakt

**9.**

This begins on the 4th beat of the bar in 4 time.

Attaque sur le 4ème temps d'une mesure à 4 temps.

Dieses Stück beginnt auf dem vierten Schlag des Taktes in einem Vierertakt.

**10.**

Count: 1 2 3

3/8 time – counting 3 (quavers/ eighth notes) in each bar.

Mesure à 3/8 – 3 pulsations (croches) par mesure.

3/8-Takt – zähle in jedem Takt auf 3 (Achtelnoten).

**11.**

**D minor** / *ré* mineur / d-Moll

## 12.

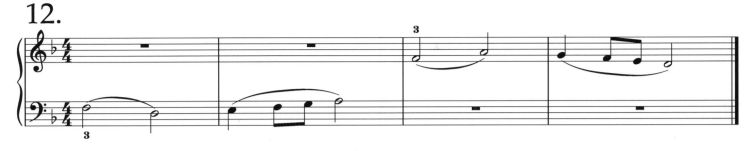

This begins on the 3rd beat of the bar in 3 time.

Attaque sur le 3ème temps d'une mesure à 3 temps.

Dieses Stück beginnt auf dem dritten Schlag des Taktes im Dreiertakt.

## 13.

This begins on the 2nd beat of the bar in 2 time.

Attaque sur le 2ème temps d'une mesure à 2 temps.

Dieses Stück beginnt auf dem zweiten Schlag des Taktes im Zweiertakt.

## 14.

This begins on the 3rd beat of the bar in 3 time.

Attaque sur le 3ème temps d'une mesure à 3 temps.

Das folgende Stück beginnt auf dem dritten Schlag des Taktes im Dreiertakt.

## 15.

# A New Hand Position
## Nouvelle position de la main
### *Eine neue Handposition*

**F major**/*fa* majeur/F-Dur

You will need to play the black-key B flats in both hands in this basic F major position, using your 4th finger in the right hand and your 2nd finger in the left hand.

Jouez le *si* bémol (touche noire) aux deux mains dans la position de base de la tonalité de *fa* majeur, avec le 4ème doigt de la main droite et le 2ème doigt de la main gauche.

In dieser Grundstellung von F-Dur muss man in beiden Händen b (schwarze Tasten) spielen, wobei man in der rechten Hand den vierten und in der linken Hand den zweiten Finger benutzt.

**1.**

**2.**

Using  in 4 time

Rythme 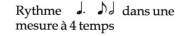 dans une mesure à 4 temps

Der Gebrauch von ♩. ♪♩ im Viertertakt.

**3.**

**F major**/*fa* majeur/F-Dur

Using ♩. ♪♩ ♩ in 4 time.

This begins on the 4th beat of the bar.

Rythme ♩. ♪♩ ♩ dans une mesure à 4 temps.

Attaque sur le 4ème temps de la mesure.

Der Gebrauch von ♩. ♪♩ ♩ im Vierertakt.

Dieses Stück beginnt auf dem vierten Schlag des Taktes.

## 4.

Count: 1 2 3

## 5.

## 6.

Count: 1 2

**F major**/*fa* majeur/F-Dur

**7.**

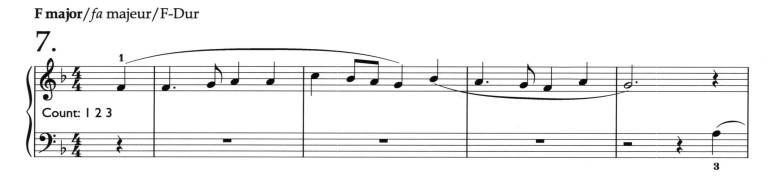

Count: 1 2 3

**8.**

**9.**

| Introducing ♩. ♫ | Introduction du rythme ♩. ♫ | Hier wird der Rhythms ♩. ♫ |
| in 3/8 ♩. ♫ | dans une mesure à 3/8 ♩. ♫ | im 3/8-Takt eingeführt ♩. ♫ |
| 1 2 and 3 | 1 2 et 3 | 1 2 und 3 |

**10.**

**F major**/*fa* majeur/F-Dur

## 11.

## A New Hand Position
## Nouvelle position de la main
### *Eine neue Handposition*

**D major**/*ré* majeur/D-Dur

You will need to play the black-key F sharps in both hands in this basic D major position. These will be under the 3rd fingers in both hands.

Jouez le *fa* dièse (touche noire) aux deux mains dans la position de base de la tonalité de *ré* majeur, avec le 3ème doigt de chaque main.

In dieser Grundstellung von D-Dur muss man in beiden Händen *fis* (schwarze Tasten) spielen. In beiden Händen wird dafür der dritte Finger benutzt.

## 1.

## 2.

**D major**/*ré* majeur/D-Dur

**3.**

**4.**

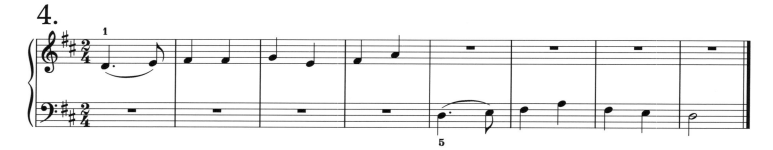

**5.**

Count: 1 2 3

**6.**

**D major**/*ré* majeur/D-Dur

**7.**

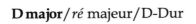

**8.**

**9.**

**D major**/*ré* majeur/D-Dur

## 10.

**Alternative G major positions to include F♯**
Autres positions en *sol* majeur avec le *fa*♯
*Alternative G-Dur Handpositionen mit fis*

## 1. Gavotte

## 2.

**3.**

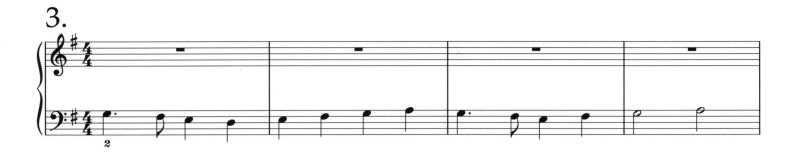

**Alternative D major positions to include C♯**
Autres positions en *ré* majeur avec le *do* ♯
*Alternative D-Dur Handpositionen mit cis*

**1.**

**2.**

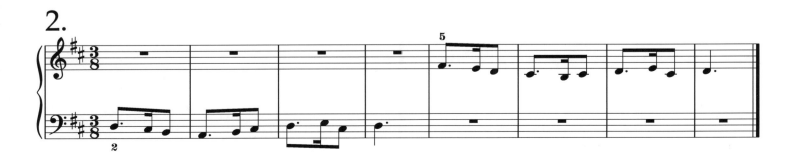

**3.**

**4.**

## A minor positions using G♯ and the melodic minor scale
Positions en *la* mineur avec le *sol♯* et la gamme mineure mélodique
*Handpositionen bei a-Moll, die das gis und die melodische Molltonleiter benutzen*

**1.**

**2.**

**3.**

**4.**

## D minor positions using C♯ and the melodic minor scale
Positions en *ré* mineur avec le *sol♯* et la gamme mineure mélodique
*Handpositionen bei d-Moll, die das cis und die melodische Molltonleiter benutzen*

**1.**

**2.**

**3.**

**4.**

# Part 2

## 2ème Partie/Teil 2

# Four Steps to Success
## Quatre étapes vers la réussite
### *Vier Schritte zum Erfolg*

From now on you will need to work out the key and hand positions for yourself.

1. **Look at the *top* number of the time signature**. Tap (clap or play on one note) the rhythm, counting all the time.

2. **Look between the clef and the time signature for any sharps or flats**. Make sure you know which notes these apply to.

3. **Look for *patterns*. While tapping,** look for any repeated notes, skips, and at the overall shape of the melody. Also look to see where you need to play the sharps or flats.

4. *Keep counting as you play*.

A partir d'ici, vous déterminerez la tonalité et la position des mains par vous-même.

1. **Observez le *chiffre supérieur* de l'indication de mesure**. Frappez le rythme (dans les mains ou sur une seule note) en comptant tous les temps.

2. **Repérez les altérations placées entre la clef et l'indication de mesure**. Assurez-vous des notes altérées.

3. **Repérez les *formules*. Tout en frappant le rythme,** repérez les notes répétées, les sauts de notes et le contour général de la mélodie. Recherchez aussi où se trouvent les notes altérées.

4. *Jouez en comptant.*

Von jetzt an musst du die Tonarten und die geeigneten Hand-positionen selbst herausfinden.

1. **Schaue dir die *obere Ziffer* der Taktangabe an**. Schlage (klatsche oder spiele auf einer Note) den Rhythmus, wobei du die ganze Zeit mitzählst.

2. **Schaue zwischen dem Notenschlüssel und der Taktangabe nach Kreuz-und B-Vorzeichen**. Sei dir sicher, dass du genau weißt, zu welchen Noten sie gehören.

3. **Achte auf *Muster*. Während du den Rhythmus schlägst,** finde alle sich wiederholenden Noten, Sprünge und die allgemeine Form der Melodie heraus.

4. *Behalte beim Spielen das Zählen des Metrums bei.*

# Introducing Intervals of 4ths and 5ths
## Introduction des intervalles de quarte et de quinte
### *Einführung der Quarte und Quinte*

Intervals of a **4th** are larger than a skip and go from line to space or space to line, and on the piano generally use fingers 2 and 5 or 1 and 4.

*Don't forget to look for the sharps and flats you need to play.*

Les intervalles de quarte sont plus grands qu'un saut de note et se lisent d'une ligne à un interligne ou d'un interligne à une ligne. On les joue généralement au piano en utilisant les doigtés 2-5 ou 1-4.

*N'oubliez pas de repérer les altérations qui y sont nécessaires.*

Das Intervall der Quarte ist größer als ein Sprung und geht von einer Notenlinie zu einem Zwischenraum oder umgekehrt. Auf dem Klavier werden dafür normalerweise die Finger 2 und 5 oder 1 und 4 benutzt.

*Vergiss dabei nicht, auf die Kreuz- und B-Vorzeichen zu achten.*

**1.**

**2.**

**3.**

Look for the 4ths before you play.     Rechercher les quartes avant de jouer.     Finde die Quarten, bevor du zu spielen anfängst.

Intervals of a 5th move from line to line or space to space and in the normal hand position use fingers 1 and 5.

Les intervalles de quinte se lisent d'une ligne à une ligne ou d'un interligne à un interligne. La position normale de la main pour les jouer utilise le doigté 1-5.

Das Quintintervall bewegt sich von Notenlinie zu Notenlinie oder von Zwischenraum zu Zwischenraum. In der normalen Handposition werden dafür die Finger 1 und 5 benutzt.

**1.**

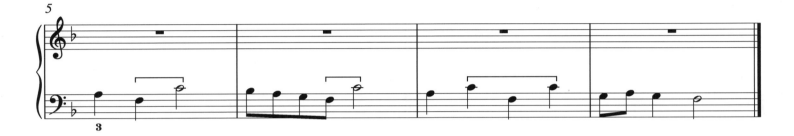

**2.**

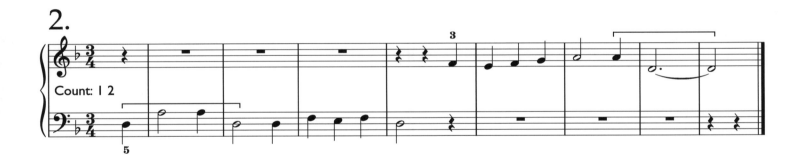

**3.**

Look for the 5ths before you play.     Rechercher les quintes avant de jouer.     Finde die Quinten, bevor du zu spielen anfängst.

**4.**

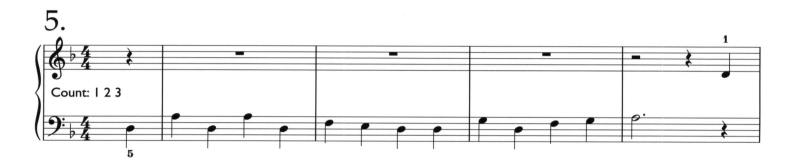

Count: 1 2 3

**5.**

Count: 1 2 3

**6.**

**7.**

# More Sight-Reading Exercises
## Nouveaux exercices de lecture à vue
### *Weitere Vom-Blatt-Spiel Übungen*

Make sure you find the correct hand positions and accidentals (sharps or flats) before you start.

Assurez-vous de la position correcte des mains et des altérations (dièses ou bémols) avant de commencer.

Vergewissere dich, dass du die richtigen Handpositionen und alle Vorzeichen (Kreuze und B) gefunden hast, bevor du anfängst.

**1. In March style**

**2. Waltz**

**3. Gently flowing**

46

## Ties and Simple Syncopations
## Liaisons et syncopes simples
### *Bindungen und einfache Synkopen*

*Remember to check the rhythm before you begin to play.*

Look out for the tied notes in nos. 5, 6 and 10, and for the syncopated rhythms in nos. 8 and 11.

*N'oubliez pas de vérifier le rythme avant de commencer à jouer.*

Repérez les notes liées dans les n° 5, 6 et 10 et les rythmes syncopés dans les n° 8 et 11.

**4.  Not too fast**

**5.  Allegretto**

**6.  Moderato**

**7.  Steadily**

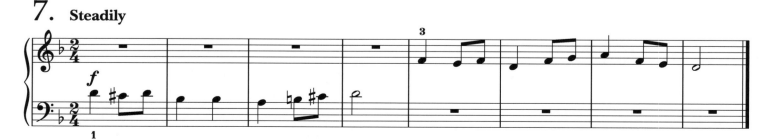

**8.** **Andante**

**9.** **Rhythmically**

**10.** **Flowing**

**11.** **Lively**

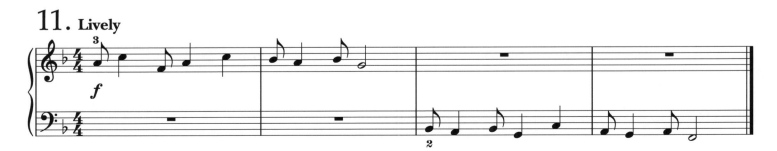

# Simple Exercises with Hands Together
## Exercices faciles à deux mains
### *Einfache Übungen mit beiden Händen*

These pieces all stay in the 5-note position.

Position de la main sur 5 notes.

Diese Stücke beschränken sich alle auf den 5-Ton-Raum.

**1. Legato**

**2. Moderato**

**3. Gently**

**4.** **Legato**

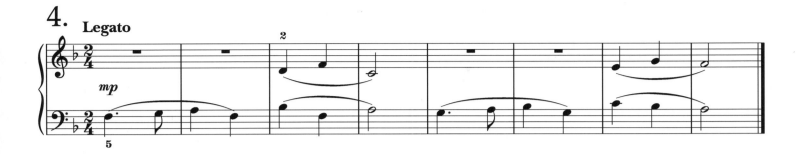

**5.** **Vivace**

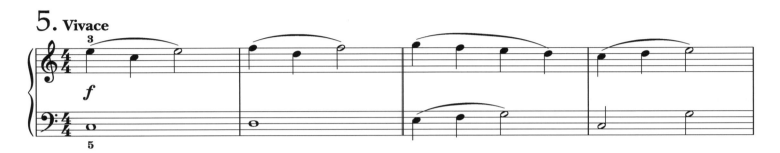

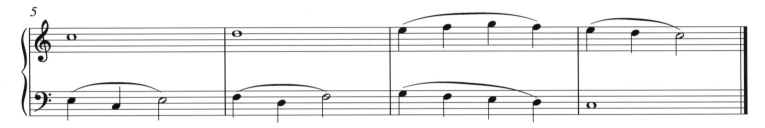

**6.** **Flowing**

**7.** **In March style**

**8.** **Lightly**

**9.** **Simply**

**10.** **Flowing**

**11.** **Vivace**

**12.** **Moderato**

**13.** **Allegretto**

**14.** **With a lilt**

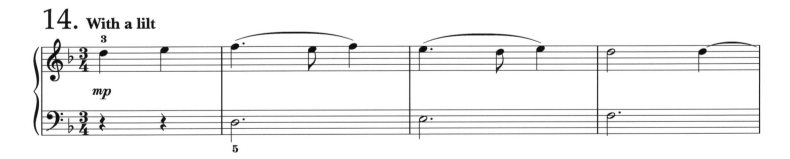

## 15. Andante

## 16. Lightly

## 17. Moderato

Schott Music Ltd, London  S&Co.7872